Home After a Long Absence:
Haiku, Senryu and Tanka

Olivier Schopfer

First Edition: 2020
Rs. 200/-

Cyberwit.net
HIG 45 Kaushambi Kunj, Kalindipuram
Allahabad - 211011 (U.P.) India
http://www.cyberwit.net
Tel: +(91) 9415091004 +(91) (532) 2552257
E-mail: info@cyberwit.net

Printed at Repro India Limited.

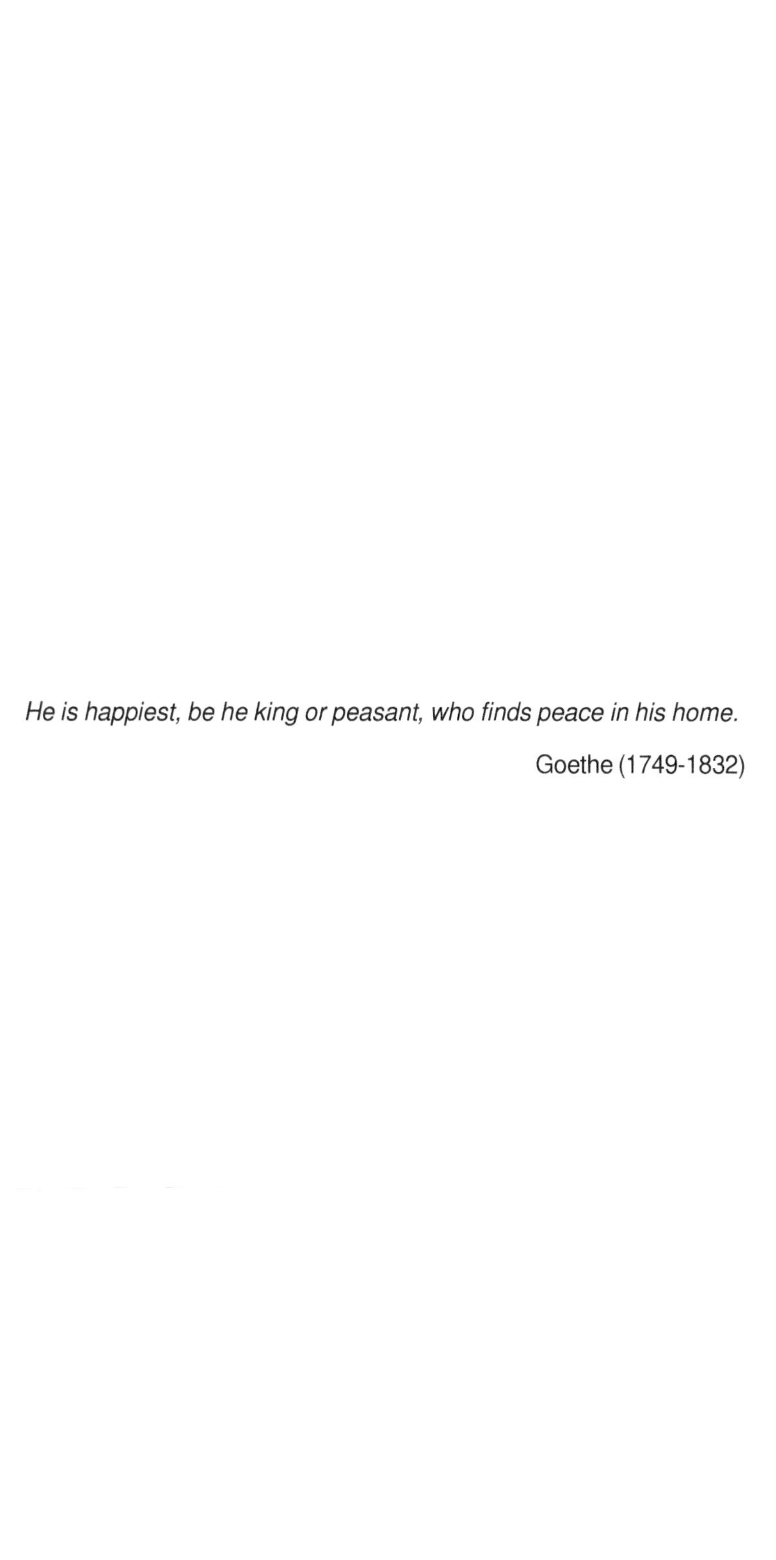

He is happiest, be he king or peasant, who finds peace in his home.

Goethe (1749-1832)

Publication Credits

Thank you to the editors of the following publications in which many of the poems in this collection first appeared, occasionally in slightly different form: *Akitsu Quarterly, All the Way Home: Aging in Haiku (Middle Island Press), Autumn Moon Haiku Journal, Bones, Bottle Rockets, Brass Bell, Cattails, Chrysanthemum, Failed Haiku, Haiku Dialogue, Haiku Windows, Haiku in the Workplace, HumanKind Journal, A Hundred Gourds, Issa's Untidy Hut: Wednesday Haiku, Modern Haiku, Naad Anunaad: an Anthology of Contemporary World Haiku (Vishwkarma Publications), Not Unaware: Short Poems on Beauty (Befuddled Press), Poets Salon, Presence, Prune Juice, Scryptic, A Sense of Place, Summer Solstice Haiku String (Australian Haiku Society), Tinywords, Under the Basho, Wales Haiku Journal, Wild Plum.*

Awards

- "afternoon stillness": *Robert Spiess Memorial Haiku Award Competition for 2016,* Honorable Mention Award.

- "sudden wind*": Vancouver Cherry Blossom Festival Haiku Invitational 2017*, honourable mention.

- "summer's end": *Russian Haiku Competition 2019*, honourable mention.

- "summer wind": *Wild Plum Haiku Contest 2019*, honorable mention.

- "patching things up": *Vancouver Cherry Blossom Festival Haiku Invitational 2019*, honourable mention.

- "magnolia buds": *Golden Haiku 2019*, selected poem.

- "all my dreams": *2019 Autumn Moon Haiku Journal, Best of Issue,* honorable mention.

- "the words": *Mainichi Haiku Contest 2019, International Section*, second prize.

- "adding milk to my tea": *Sharpening the Green Pencil Haiku Contest 2020*, third honorable mention.

home after
a long absence
lilacs in bloom

mountaintop at dusk
one after another
in the valley
the village houses
light up

sudden wind
the garden buddha's head crowned
with cherry blossoms

no translation needed robin's song

bitter dispute
the washer goes into
its spin-dry cycle

patching things up
cherry blossoms scattered
over our doorstep

walking down a different street
to get home
my whole day changed

all the birds' reborn songs spring sunshine

still life
a housefly lands
on the sliced apple

watering orchids
the inside
of a cat's ear

stretching out
on the living room floor
the cat and a sunbeam

not seeing them
until it is too late
window cleaners

billowing
the bedroom curtains out
spring breeze

round the corner
a new asphalt driveway
dental scaling day

clip-clop
clip-clop
cobblestones

spring cleaning
the cassette player
that chewed up tapes

treasures and trash parts of me

wildflower meadow
the invisible life
of soil organisms

night rain
with each car passing
splashing waves

after the storm
the gurgle of rain
in the drainpipe

magnolia buds
about to open
new friendship

breakfast
alighting on
the window sill
a sparrow
with a twig in its beak

still no reply
steam escapes
the tea kettle

adding milk to my tea
the many shapes
of morning clouds

for a short
very short moment
everything
seems possible
summer stars

heat wave
black dots
all over the flypaper

picnic
the bottles we put
in the river to cool

skipping stones
the difference between
stressed and unstressed syllables

sunrise
the fruit bowl
full of oranges

twilight
from the window box
the scent of lavender

in from the garden
an ant
makes its way through
the labyrinth
of my forearm hair

too many paths
we stray off
the way home

summer wind taking shape clothesline

first drops of rain
halfway up the wild rose stem
a ladybird stops

a brief pause before
making a mess of it
strawberry millefeuille

afternoon stillness
a cricket leaps
out of its shadow

summer's end
the bruised skin
of overripe peaches

last sunset
of the summer
the slow flapping of its wings
as a swan
flies away

family cookbook
stained
and filled
with pencilled notes
autumn dusk

frost
on the kitchen window
smell of freshly brewed coffee

morning drizzle
bacon strips
sizzling in the frying pan

home alone
the slanting rays
of the late afternoon sun

pouring rain
the buttery texture
of red kuri squash

hazy morning
the sound of the knife blade
being sharpened

all the birds' lost songs autumn wind

migrating swallows
for a moment
the sky darkens

nightfall
a stray cat
follows us home

faded ink
on an old friend's postcard
I used to know
how to write
in cursive

mist over the river
the blank page fills
with haiku

no message
on my answering machine
rising fog

if only...
the dreams
under my pillow

the long parentheses of insomnia

in front of the grocery store
a homeless man
asking for change

depending on what I do today tomorrow

the time between
realisation
and acceptance
full moon

first cold day
hard to the touch
the avocado skin

hot topic
the cheese soufflé
deflates

fallen leaves
pages of my haiku book
coming loose from the spine

November wind
the familiar squeak
of the rusty weathervane

morning clouds
the geometric flight
of cormorants

on my welcome doormat
an unwelcome salesman

phoning my aged mother
the time it takes her
to answer

disorder
arranged
bed throw pillows

dusty cushions
the illusions
I cling to

all my dreams
not come true
winter stars

waking up
the world so quiet
fresh snow

the pleasure
of getting in the mail
something
other than bills
overseas postcard

(for Elizabeth Crocket)

flu season my infected computer

wild wind
the promise
I will not keep

television crime drama
I double
lock my door

today's news
turning on the television
with the sound off

the outdated comfort
of a hot-water bottle
alone tonight

hail knocking
on the glass roof
my loneliness

frozen to the bone
in my takeout bag
hot spring rolls

gibbous moon
the last jigsaw puzzle piece
added to the picture

confinement
my neighbourhood
the whole world

isolation my inner landscape

ticking clock
the time
inside the snow globe

all day sun
the remains
of the snowman

just an excuse
to kiss you
mistletoe

in the dark of the kitchen
with the fridge door open
winter solstice

watching
the neighbours having fun
New Year's Eve

break of day
one more verbal blow
from my shakespearean insults calendar

the words
I should have said
dying embers

smell of cut grass
from the nextdoor neighbour's lawn
moving day

moving out
where the pictures used to hang
brighter spots